SEVEN TO EIGHT INCOME/INVESTMENT STREAMS

SEVEN TO EIGHT INCOME/INVESTMENT STREAMS

LEST THE LAND BECOME DESOLATE

COLLEEN E. EDWARDS

Copyright © 2020 by Colleen E. Edwards.

Library of Congress Control Number: 2020905384
ISBN: Hardcover 978-1-7960-9508-1
Softcover 978-1-7960-9509-8
eBook 978-1-7960-9526-5

All rights reserved. No part of this book may be reproduced or transmitted in any form or by any means, electronic or mechanical, including photocopying, recording, or by any information storage and retrieval system, without permission in writing from the copyright owner.

The views expressed in this work are solely those of the author and do not necessarily reflect the views of the publisher, and the publisher hereby disclaims any responsibility for them.

Any people depicted in stock imagery provided by Getty Images are models, and such images are being used for illustrative purposes only. Certain stock imagery © Getty Images.

Print information available on the last page.

Rev. date: 03/20/2020

To order additional copies of this book, contact:
Xlibris
1-888-795-4274
www.Xlibris.com
Orders@Xlibris.com
811291

DEDICATION

To my nephew Jabari Natty for giving me the NIV version of the Bible, Christmas 2017, as my Christmas Gift. It was after reading this version of the Bible that Ecclesiastes 11: 1-2 became plain to me that our Lord wanted us to have 7-8 investments/income streams lest the land becomes desolate.

Thanks nephew, for the man of God that you have become. Continued success as you grow in the Lord.

To my nephew Rohan Slacks, Sr., you have become a businessman and a hard-working entrepreneur. I see the word of God coming alive to you as you master your various businesses. Much success to you as you explore new ideas and new ventures.

To my sisters Olive Edwards, Shirley Edwards, and Lorraine Myers. Thank you for being there through thick and thin, good times and bad. Have great success in life.

ACKNOWLEDGMENTS

To my spiritual parents, Bishop Henry Fernandez and Pastor Carol Fernandez, thank you for your continued blessing to us at The Faith Center. Your amazing faith in God has been passed down to the congregation. I am forever grateful as you continue to let the Lord use you. You are the light on the hill that we need here in Sunrise, FL, and around the world.

To Errol Bovell, Dexter Laughton, Moses Wright, Norice Matthews, Kelly Bryan, and Anthony Jacques, your contribution over the years of Real Estate advice, Insurance advice, Forex market advice has been priceless, and I am forever grateful for your input. Much success to you in your many ventures.

To Joan Prince, Michelle Richards-Phillips, Carleen Richards, Doreen Wallace, Lorna Brown, and Charmain Brown, the friends in my life that are always there.

Thank you for your contribution.

ENDORSEMENTS

You did it again Colleen this book is written from not just a place of research but as a testimony for the investments that you have made. I remember when we invested in Real Estate together and you used that passion and experience to help others. Only a true Woman of God like yourself would do that. I recommend this as a great read the different investment option The fact that you even went back to basics to remind them not to forget jobs but use it as a stepping stone to become an Entrepreneur .... God bless you on this book Colleen and I just cannot wait on the launch ... #gglloorryy

Evangelist Michelle Richards-Phillips

Colleen you have done it again, congratulations!!!

Another self help book, teaching the many the essentials of how to navigate the world of finance and business through investing and money management. Your book will educate and inspire success You have been my mentor on many things

May I thank you!!!

Moses Wright, Businessman & Investor

FOREWORD

This book is an embodiment of the author, Colleen Edwards, she lives her life striving to be the best she can be. Her life's experience, faith, education and career, has brought her to these focal points.

Her belief in certain principles of the Bible and the concept of America The Free has led her to belive in having choices. The material in this book, Seven sources of income, comes from the heart backed by logic and the word. Providing a shared vision for those individuals who want to improve their lot in life.

Finally, the true beneficiaries of these ideas are the future generations of the persons adopting them.

Errol Bovell, President
EDB Financial Services

INTRODUCTION

On December 25, 2017, my nephew gave me a New International Version (NIV) Bible for my Christmas gift. He had purchased Bibles for every adult family member with our names engraved on the cover.

I thought this is a nice gift. Before this, I had only read the King James Version of the Bible. I started reading my new Bible on January 1, 2018, and had a goal to read the entire Bible by the end of the year. I accomplished my goal. It is quite interesting that I have been reading the Bible since childhood, and certain scriptures did not jump out at me until I read the NIV version of the Bible.

One scripture that jumped off the pages was Ecclesiastes 11: 2. The scripture reads, "Invest in seven ventures, yes in eight, you do not know what disaster may come upon the land. "It was like the lights came on. If you read my book "Tithes & Offerings an Act of Love," you heard my story how much we lost when the economy took a downturn in 2008. It took a while to recover but thanks be to almighty God, he has restored us over and over again.

Now, what is the word saying to us here, diversify your investments my people so if disaster comes you will be able to survive.

So with this revelation, this book is written to bless you. Read and act. The desire of the Lord is for you to prosper and be in good health.

Contents

Chapter 1 Real Estate, Real Estate, Real Estate 1
   Fix And Flip Properties 1
   Buy And Hold Properties 2
   Wholesaling Real Estate 2
   Pre-Construction Properties 2
   Commercial Real Estate 3
   Invest In Land 3

Chapter 2 Stocks & Bonds 7

Chapter 3 Foreign Exchange Trading 9
   Currency Trading 9
   Metatrader 4 .Oanda.forex.com 9
   Trading Currencies 10

Chapter 4 Cryptocurrencies 11
   Crypto Craft 12

Chapter 5 Your Gifts / Your Talent 13
   Import/Exports 13
   Farming 14
   Pre-School 14
   Multi-Level Marketing/ Direct Marketing 14
   Online Marketing 15
   Natural Born Gifts And Talents 16
   Singers 16
   Songwriters 16
   Band Members 17

Writers 17
　　　Inventions 18
　　　Sports 20
　　　Handyman or Woman/ Contractors &
　　　　　Sub-Contractors 20
　　　Landscaping Business 21

Chapter 6　The Job Working 9 To 5 23

Chapter 7　Life Insurance & Annuities 27

Chapter 8　Investing in the Kingdom of God 31

CHAPTER 1

REAL ESTATE, REAL ESTATE, REAL ESTATE

I arose one early morning and heard this whispered in my ear, "Real Estate, Real Estate, Real Estate." I jumped up and asked Lord, what are you trying to tell me.

I started looking over what I have been working on all year. I have been a believer in multiple streams of income for some time now; however, some investments work, and some don't. I started reflecting on what has worked over the years.

I have concluded that if you are going to become wealthy, investing in Real Estate is a must. There are many ways to make money investing in Real Estate, and I will name a few here.

FIX AND FLIP PROPERTIES

You can acquire a property in need of repair, fix, and flip the property. There are so many videos, workshops, and classes on this strategy that if you are not doing this, you can start today. This strategy can be very lucrative, so do not miss out on this opportunity.

BUY AND HOLD PROPERTIES

You can buy and hold a property. This will be your rental property. There are also many video classes, videos, or simply browsing Facebook, may provide many offers on this strategy if you need the knowledge.

WHOLESALING REAL ESTATE

Wholesaling Real Estate is a strategy used by many investors. The concept is simple, buy low and sell at retail. If you are a new investor with little money to buy property, this is a technique you should investigate. There are many videos online and many articles written about wholesaling Real Estate. There are also many wholesalers on Facebook, and you can gain knowledge there. Do the research and decide if this is a strategy that fits your goals and plans for making money in Real Estate.

PRE-CONSTRUCTION PROPERTIES

Pre-Construction properties are one of my favorite strategies. If you invest in a pre-construction property at the beginning of the project in a market where prices are increasing, by the time the builder is done with your home, the property could increase substantially. I have invested in pre-construction properties that increased $50,000-$80,000 by the time the home is completed.

This is why it is good while the property is being built; you are not making payments, and the equity is increasing in the home.

The key here is to get in as soon as the builder breaks ground on that project.

Where can you find these projects? Just google pre-construction homes and type in the area that you are interested in, several projects will pop up, you can also google various builders, and the projects will come up. A few builders are, Lennar, D.R. Horton, Pulte Homes.

COMMERCIAL REAL ESTATE

An area to research is investing in Commercial Properties. Do you know that investing in Commercial properties can be very lucrative? Tenants in Commercial Properties are usually long-term tenants. e.g. a building that I worked in for 14 years, they co- leased the property for 20 years.

INVEST IN LAND

Invest in land. We need land to build, so this should be a part of your portfolio.

There are other real estate investment strategies out there, get the knowledge.

Do not limit yourself. Do not say I don't have the money. There are hard money lenders out there that are willing to loan you money if the investment makes sense. They are qualifying the investment property, not yourself, so do not use the excuse that "my credit is bad." If you have bad credit, some agencies will help you fix your credit.

No excuses, do something! One thing I like to do in my spare time is to review the Forbes Billionaire list. I am not impressed with the people that got on the list through inheritance. I am impressed with the self-made billionaire.

One thing I have noticed with the self-made Billionaire, though they may have obstacles along the way they keep trying. They do not give up easily. Another observation is that Real Estate investing has generated several self-made billionaires.

In my early twenties, I was still living in California and decided to buy my first property. What motivated me to do this was the house my mother and the family rented for several years. A new owner bought the house and wanted to live in the house, so we had to move.

When I calculated how much we had spent in rent the years we lived in the house, it totaled approximately $70,000. I thought, how unfortunate, we spent all this money over these years, and someone could just come and give us notice to leave. We had no ownership in the house after those many years and over $70,000 spent. I did not have much money then, however, I had a few thousand dollars in my 401K.

I contacted a Realtor, and we started looking at homes. It took a long time because I only had $5,000 for a down payment. I had to look outside of Los Angeles because the Los Angeles area was too expensive. After several months of looking, I found a townhouse. The Realtor was patient with me. The Townhouse was filthy, dirty, and needed painting. The carpet was so dirty, and it had changed color. However, the townhouse was in a nice area and near a very nice mall in West Covina, California.

I was talking to an older woman at the Bank where I worked, and I told her about the property. I told her that the property was so filthy that I was thinking of not getting it. This woman advised me to buy the property. She said you could invest a few thousand dollars in painting, change the carpet, and have someone professionally clean the property. To paint, change the carpet and clean it cost me $2,500.

I purchased the property and did what this older woman told me to do. We painted, changed the carpet, and had a professional come to clean. I could not believe the transformation after it was completed. We moved into that townhouse, and after two years, I sold the property. My net cash after cost and Realtor fees on that property was over $40,000.

Let me speak to the first-time home buyer here. I am a Realtor in addition to the many other things that I do. I have a few licenses; one is a Real Estate License. The most cherished license I ever got. I keep it active no matter what else I am doing. My experience with the average first-time homebuyer is that they have a small budget. This is true most of the time, for younger persons, just starting.

My advice if it is a small budget, strictly buy what you can afford. After a few years, for the most part, you would have built up some equity in the property. You can then sell and upgrade to another property. Some of my clients take this advice, and you have some who want to wait until they save up enough to get what I refer to as the mansion on the hill.

My experience with the clients who want to wait, they hardly ever get there. Do you know why? While they are saving to get the more expensive property, the prices of the homes are going up! They cannot save enough to get that house on the hill because the longer they wait, the more this dream escapes them.

It is better to start with what you can afford, build up some equity, sell, and buy what you want. Whatever you do, make sure Real Estate is a part of your portfolio.

CHAPTER 2

STOCKS & BONDS

Stocks and bonds should be a part of your investment portfolio. Now lately, the stock market has been very volatile; however, you can still make money investing in the stock market. Call a stockbroker to receive advice or contact a financial planner.

Some vehicles are:

>Roth Ira's
>Mutual Funds
>Bond funds
>Stock options

By no means am I giving investment advice here, I am encouraging you to contact the expert who will guide you to the right investment for you. One of my favorite sayings is, do not leave money on the table. There are some reference materials I would like to mention here.

Kiplinger Magazine

This magazine is a good source for researching various stocks with great articles. I have been subscribing to the Kiplinger magazine for years. Bloomberg has a TV channel that talks about the stock market all day and night. You can contact Fidelity Investments for advice.

Get the information, do not limit yourself. Look into the international and domestic stock market. Some areas are doing better than others, get knowledge.

The good thing about stocks versus real estate, you can sell a stock in a matter of seconds.

Therefore, while real estate is a long-term strategy, stocks and bonds are a liquid asset. If you need cash fast, you can get it from your stocks and bonds quicker than from Real Estate. If you have a job and you are not investing in the company's 401K plan for you, I say you are leaving money on the table. In most, if not all, 401K plans, the company will match your investment up to a certain percent of your contribution.

For example, companies I have worked with provide a match of up to 7% of what you contribute. Why not take advantage of this gift. As I mentioned in the chapter on Real Estate, the down payment for my first property came from my 401K. I cannot emphasize enough; do not let this money pass you by. Invest in the 401K if offered on your job.

CHAPTER 3

FOREIGN EXCHANGE TRADING

CURRENCY TRADING

If you have not looked into this area of investing, I would like you to start today. The field of foreign exchange trading is big, high, wide, and lucrative if you take the time to learn what this area of trading is all about.

Currency trading is simply the buying and selling of the currency. However, you do not have to get the various currencies to hold them and sell them physically. You can accomplish all of this using your computer or phone.

All you need is a trading platform and a broker to trade.

The platform I use, which can be easily installed on your phone is:

METATRADER 4 .OANDA.FOREX.COM

You will also need a broker to deposit your cash to start trading. There are many brokers out there; you can do your research and select the one that meets your needs.

There are classes you will need to take to learn how to trade currencies. I looked into classes a few years ago, and some of the Trading Academies are expensive. However, I was introduced to a company named iMarketslive a few years ago and acquired the knowledge at a fairly reasonable monthly fee.

Google iMarketslive, and do your research on this trading academy. There are also many videos online; you can watch to learn about currency trading.

TRADING CURRENCIES

FUTURES TRADING
TRADE GOLD AND SILVER

Bloomberg TV is another great source of information on foreign exchange Trading. FOREX FACTORY is another great source of information regarding the various currency pairs, you can Google FOREX FACTORY to learn more.

CHAPTER 4

CRYPTOCURRENCIES

If you have never heard the term Crypto Currencies, I want you to google this information right away. Learn as much as you can about it because this is our present and future, and they are here to stay.

WHAT IS CRYPTOCURRENCY?

Cryptocurrency is a digital asset designed to work as a medium of exchange that uses cryptography to secure financial transactions. The Bitcoin sometimes called the grandfather of the cryptocurrencies, is the most popular right now. To name a few that are amongst the most popular see below:

BITCOIN ETHERIUM IOTA RIPPLE LITECOIN

There are many videos on YouTube that you can watch to learn more about cryptocurrencies. You can also check the **World Coin Index** to see the daily news on these currencies and what they are worth daily. To buy and sell cryptocurrencies, you will need to set up a wallet. One of the more popular wallets is through **Coinbase**.

You can Google **Coinbase** to see what is required for you to set up your wallet to buy and sell cryptocurrencies. There are other wallets out there that you can explore, **COINBASE** is just one that I use.

Remember the chapter on Foreign Exchange Trading, well, you can also trade cryptocurrencies. FOREX FACTORY has created a new site just for Cryptocurrency trading called Crypto Craft.

CRYPTO CRAFT

If you decide to trade Cryptocurrencies, this is the site to go to for indicators whether you should buy or sell Cryptocurrencies. There is so much that is still unknown regarding cryptocurrencies; however, this is one avenue of investment that you should explore. Cryptocurrencies have become a global market; the world is using virtual currencies, so do not let this elude you.

CHAPTER 5

YOUR GIFTS / YOUR TALENT

What is your skill set? What do you enjoy, what talents were you born with? This area has endless possibilities. Get a Journal, start writing goals and dates you would like to accomplish these goals. Write down the strengths of your skillset. What do you enjoy?

Have you thought of opening a business? Read the Forbes Billionaire list; they publish them every year. Get ideas, read the stories. Focus on the self-made billionaires. Get familiar with what they did to get to Billionaire status.

Some areas to explore:

IMPORT/EXPORTS

What can you ship overseas? Use the internet; do research. Check on what is profitable vs. not profitable. Look at market trends, what are other people doing. How can I market a unique product or capitalize on products that are already doing well?

FARMING

This is an area to explore. We need fruits, vegetables, ginger, yams, the list goes on. Some people are good in this area, and they love planting and reaping. This is an area to explore. If you are good in this area, then work on it. Do your research, and the possibilities are endless.

PRE-SCHOOL

This is an area that is in demand and can be very profitable. There is a need for good pre-schools. If you are talented in this area, then this is a business to consider.

MULTI-LEVEL MARKETING/ DIRECT MARKETING

Some of the most successful persons in the U.S.A. and overseas made their money in an MLM as they are defined. Direct Marketing is what these businesses are called. If you have not looked into this area, you can start now. This is not for everybody; however, some of us at one point in our lives have been a part of a Multi-Level Marketing business. I have made some money when most needed in Multi-Level Marketing.

Another aspect associated with these businesses was the self-development and discipline it takes to be successful in this type of business. I am going to name a few that I have either been associated with or know to be a successful business.

AMWAY

LEGAL SHIELD

IMARKETS LIVE

MELALEUCA

TLC (Total Life Changes)

It has been years since I actively worked the Legal Shield business, and I still get residual income from the work I put in years ago. My niece is a stay at home mom who runs her Melaleuca business from home. It has been years since I actively worked the Amway business; however, I still use some of the great products that they offer. This is an area to explore. I have personally known people that have made six-figure incomes and even some millionaires as multi-level marketers.

If this is an area that you feel you could be good at, then do not hesitate to go for it. The advantage of starting this type of business you usually only need a few hundred dollars to start. Some of the most valuable business contacts and friends that I have today I met in the Multi-Level Marketing business.

ONLINE MARKETING

Persons are making a living as online marketers. Whatever you need, you can find it online. Find out what you can sell online. This is an area that can be very lucrative with minimal costs. You do not have to rent space and deal with a lot of employees.

Online marketing can also take your business worldwide. Explore this area of earning a living.

NATURAL BORN GIFTS AND TALENTS

Some persons were born with natural gifts and talents. If you are one of the fortunate to be born with a gift and you are not using that gift, I am here to encourage you to let go of what is holding you back. It may be fear, lack of funds, life events. I do not know your story; I am just here as a vessel to help you to make the best of your God-given gifts and talents.

SINGERS

Some of you can sing, use your gift to bless others, and bless yourself. Get up now, explore the endless possibilities. You may need to enter a singing competition, sing in your church, just do not only sing in the shower. Get out there and let the world know God has blessed you with a gift.

SONGWRITERS

I admire Songwriters. Have you ever explored this idea? We need you to write the next song. Consult with good Songwriters, find out how they got started. I am certain they were not all born with this gift. This is an area that can be developed.

BAND MEMBERS

Now we need more keyboard players, drummers, saxophone players, violinists, percussion, and band members. You can make a living using your gift. Find out where you are needed and apply.

WRITERS

Is it possible that you have a story to tell? You may be a writer. Let go of fear and start writing. I know it is somewhat intimidating if you have never written a book before. When I wrote my first book, a children's book titled "Lost in the Woods," I had sleepless nights from the time I started writing the book to the day the book was published. I had thoughts going through my mind that no one would like the book, maybe it was not such a good idea after all.

Even though I had it in mind for some years that I wanted to write a children's book because I enjoyed reading these books as a child, I wanted to give back to an area that I enjoyed as a child. It was not easy; however, I overcame fear and published the book.

Needless to say, it has been one of the most rewarding accomplishments in my life. I went on to write my second book, "Tithes & Offerings an Act of Love," a book that I felt I was blessed to write and am very proud of that book. I said all of this to encourage you if you have a book or books in you start today. Get around the computer and start writing. There are persons out there to help you edit and publish your book.

INVENTIONS

One day I was sitting at my desk; I was sending an email. I thought about what we would do without email. Soon after a friend called me and I said to the friend, have you thought about how much easier our lives have become because of the persons that invented something. Just email, for instance. Do you know the reason companies can allow employees to work from home is because of email, the computer, and the phone?

We started going down the list:

Email

Television

Cell Phone

Facebook

Refrigerator

Electric Stove

Computers

Printers

Post-it Notes

Cars

Airplane

Electricity

Washer & Dryer

Eyeglasses

Contact Lenses

I could go on and on. Check the billionaire list. The inventors came up with an invention to make human life easier, and the money followed them. What are you inventing? What have you thought of? Look around you what can you create to make human life easier. There are endless possibilities out there. Start thinking. Get a notepad to start jotting ideas down. Do your research. What else could we use to make our lives easier? Are you the next inventor?

I want to mention here that some of the most useful products are from persons who may not have been the original inventor; however, the enhancements they have developed have made the product more compact, more useful than the invention. I remember when cell phones were first introduced, they were huge compared to the cell phones of today. The televisions are now flat-screen TV's, much different from what they were originally. I could go on and on. So even if you are not the original inventor, what can you do to enhance an appliance, the computer, the cell phone. There are many items to develop.

SPORTS

Other areas to consider are Basketball players, football players, Hockey Players, Track & Field, Soccer, and Tennis, to name a few. Some of you are gifted in the sports arena; however, because of life circumstances, you have not been able to use your gift. Let me encourage you to do whatever it takes to move forward with your gift.

Mothers and Fathers, if you recognize a gifted child, do what you can to develop this gift. Do research, connect with the right people to help you.

HANDYMAN OR WOMAN/ CONTRACTORS & SUB-CONTRACTORS

Some of you are good with your hands, and you fix things. We need plumbers, tile and wood flooring persons, electricians, roofers, painters, air conditioning persons, cabinet workers.

You may not have gone to college, but you are good with your hands. Start your business today. Find out what you need to do to be licensed and insured. Make up some business cards and start your business. We need you.

Many investors are fixing and flipping properties that are looking for good workers. Cities are looking for good contractors and sub-contractors to do work, to give you a contract. Did you know that a lot of the work that is done in the area the Cities hire Contractors to do the work? Find out what it takes to get these contracts. There are additional areas to explore.

LANDSCAPING BUSINESS

This is a lucrative business waiting for you to start if you are gifted in this area. You are in demand, especially where we live in South Florida.

CHAPTER 6

THE JOB WORKING 9 TO 5

Most of us after college or high school were taught to get a job. We, as a society, tend to complain about the job, the 9-5. I want you to change your mindset as you read this book about the job. See this way of making money as a great way to start building wealth. I appreciate the job.

With the job, you get a steady income, for the most part, every two weeks or every week. You have health benefits, 401K, pension, and life insurance benefits. It is how you handle the money you make on the job that counts. How you invest this money to make it work for you.

Real Estate Agents and Mortgage Brokers love the clients with a good job, a steady income. It is easier for you to qualify for a loan if you show the stability that a steady income provides.

Some business owners got their experience on the job. After the work experience, many have opened up their own business.

You may work on a 9-5 job until retirement. Again it's what you do with the money you make. If you are getting ready to go to college, I would advise you to do your research to see what jobs are paying the most money. Use this to the best of your ability.

Sign on to Indeed.com or Career Builders.com and search jobs. See what qualifications you need to get the highest paying job. Work towards the qualification you need to get the job.

All are not going to be business owners, and we need the employee to make the business work. The employees play an important role in our society.

From this day forward, I want you to look at your job as a stepping stone to build wealth. Use your money wisely. Do you wonder how some persons are making the same money you are making, and they seem to be progressing much more than others? These employees are investing their money wisely.

Most companies offer a 401K with a company match. I am amazed at some persons who do not participate in the 401K on their job. This is like allowing free money to go by the wayside. One of my favorite sayings is do not leave money on the table. Not participating in the 401K on your job is throwing away money.

Under the chapter in this book dedicated to real estate investing, you will note where I got the down payment for that first property. I purchased it from my 401K. The 401K is intended to go towards your retirement savings; however, when I purchased that first property, I was in my early twenties, a long way from retirement. Purchasing that property was a start to future investments that have been nothing short of amazing profits.

Some jobs have pensions. I have a pension from two former employers, another benefit of having a job.

Some companies offer tuition reimbursement. This may not be as popular as in the past, but I am sure some companies still offer tuition reimbursement.

I worked at a bank at the age of 18 that offered tuition reimbursement as long as I got a grade of C or better in school. I participated in this program and was able to get a portion of my college education funded by my employer. Do your research, find out what companies are offering tuition reimbursement. If you are still in school, you may want to seek employment in a company that offers tuition reimbursement.

So from this day forward, if you are an employee, I am advising you to make the best of it. This is the way most persons earn money in our society today. Have a positive outlook on the job. Use this vehicle to make money to the best of your ability. Invest wisely and watch your money grow.

CHAPTER 7

LIFE INSURANCE & ANNUITIES

A good man leaves an inheritance for his children's children. We hear this quote all the time, but have we considered what this is telling us. If you do not have a life insurance policy, you should consider meeting with a Life Insurance Agent as soon as possible to see what your options are. Policies today are much more flexible than policies in the past.

We now have the option of choosing Universal Life policies with living benefits. What are living benefits? These are policies that you do not have to die to benefit from them. They have critical illness riders that if you are diagnosed with a critical illness, and you survive, you can get cash from the policy to pay your bills while you are recovering.

In my field, as an Insurance Adjuster and Life Insurance agent, I have seen cases over and over again young, middle-aged, and elderly who get a critical illness and cannot work for a while.

We do not want to face the inevitable, but we know that one day we will pass on. This event does not care if you are young, middle-aged, or old. A friend of mine just recently lost her son, a young man in his early 30's. After his death, his sister posted on Facebook to get life insurance because death does not care that you are young.

On a more positive note, some life policies have a cash value. Some people have started businesses by accessing money from their life insurance policies.

If all you have is a term policy on your job, I would advise you to contact a Life Insurance agent today to see what you can acquire on your own.

I worked at a company for 14 years, and when they moved out of town, and I could not go with them, I lost my Life Insurance benefit from that company. It is a good thing I was knowledgeable enough to get a policy on my own when I was younger, so when they left, I had some form of coverage.

If you are telling yourself that you cannot afford the monthly premium for a Life Insurance policy, you may not know that there are very affordable plans out there. I know we like to look nice; we drive nice cars; we spend money on hair and hairdos. Especially if you have children, you should be thinking about their future.

The designer clothes and tennis shoes should not be a priority. The Lord showed me clearly if you desire to be in lack, you are selfish. The poor cannot help the poor. Leave a legacy for your family, your church, your favorite charity. Help someone along the way. Cover yourself, critical illnesses are a reality, unfortunately, and they have no mercy and do not respect age. Young, old, middle-aged falls into this category.

Life insurance policies again is a form of income for you and your family.

ANNUITIES

What are annuities?

An annuity is a vehicle to create retirement income and defer year-end taxes. There are many annuity products available. With so many options, it is best to get with an agent who can explain the different options, and you can determine if an annuity is right for you and which one.

If you are interested in protecting your savings from loss but want to grow your savings without the risk that comes with the volatility of the stock market, a fixed indexed annuity may be right for you.

If you are looking for security and lifetime income, then an annuity may be the right choice for you.

Again, get knowledge. Whether you choose this vehicle of investment or not, at least look into it.

CHAPTER 8

INVESTING IN THE KINGDOM OF GOD

The best investment you can make is giving back after you have made all the money in the seven investments, we covered in the last seven chapters. Examples of how you can give, you can start with your church. In my book Tithes & Offerings an Act of Love, I talk about paying your tithes. You can get a copy of that book on AMAZON.COM. You can give to charity and the poor.

Poor cannot help poor; however, if you have enough after your obligations are taken care of, you can bless others. It is the principle of sowing and reaping. The Bible says, "give and it shall be given unto you," Luke 6:38 KJV. The Lord showed me; clearly, he is not blessing us to buy a big house and a nice car. He is blessing us to be a blessing to those in need.

What has the Lord prepared us for, everything we need is in the word. Ecclesiastes 11: 1-2 talks about the seven to eight investments you need to have lest the land become desolate. This is how we will survive to help ourselves and our families in times of economic downturn and disasters. When I attended college in business school, we talked about diversifying our portfolio. This is the discussion we are having in this book.

The main goal is to get you to change your mindset, from which I can only do one thing. Working for a paycheck is fine for a while; however, what you do with that paycheck will lead you to financial freedom. I read the scripture Ecclesiastes for years "cast your bread upon the waters, and it may return in many days," and I did not know what this scripture meant.

The purpose of this book is not to give you financial advice. Some Financial Advisors are trained in this field to guide you. The purpose of this book is to reveal to you what the Lord intended in Ecclesiastes 11: 1-2, to prepare us for what may come. The advice is to invest in seven to eight ventures in case of a disaster that may come upon the land.

As I was writing this book, a devastating hurricane named Dorian hit Abaco and Freeport, Bahamas. This storm caused many to lose their home, become homeless; some even lost loved ones. Another event that has impacted the world is the Corona virus. COVD-19. The world has gone on lock down because of this virus. We have seen schools, churches and businesses close. The stock market has tumbled and as I am writing this book the world is scrambling to find a vaccine. People are losing their lives and jobs are laying off daily. Most are not prepared for this type of event.

If this book accomplishes what it is intended to accomplish, it would have changed your mindset to thinking I can do more than one money-making activity. There are seven other investment opportunities out there for me. Start exploring your wealth today. Start with research on the internet. There is so much information on the internet. Even on Facebook, there are so many persons talking about what they are investing in, tap into this information.

I did not say seven jobs. Investments are what you should explore. Stop using excuses that you don't have money to invest. You do, rearrange what you are doing. You don't need 60 pairs of shoes. It is alright to wear what you have in your closet, mix, and match, and you may have to give up purchasing an outfit every week or every time you get paid. You have to start sometime. I am here to encourage you to begin today.

We just rang in the new year, 2020, and I am looking at my calendar, and we are on day nine.

Time may pass you by if you do not start today. Start where you are, do not procrastinate. We can say tomorrow; I will do something. I am here to encourage you to start today.

I am looking forward to hearing great success stories after your reading of this very important book. I give all the credit to God for giving us such a great manual, the Bible. I thank my nephew once again for giving me the gift of the word of God, Christmas 2017.

www.ingramcontent.com/pod-product-compliance
Lightning Source LLC
Chambersburg PA
CBHW031502210526
45463CB00003B/1044